Basically...

By Katelyn Dalton

DEDICATION

First, I have to thank my mom for having an awesome brother who is coincidentally my favorite uncle. And thanks, Dad, for everything--especially having an amazing brother-in-law, who also is coincidentally my favorite uncle. You're my favorite parents ever.

CONTENTS

ACKNOWLEDGMENTS

I didn't realize how much fun I had with the English language until I read "Irregardless," the book my uncle and cousin wrote. I wanted to be just like them and write a book, and he's so amazing that he agreed to help me put my book together. Thanks, Uncle Ken, for helping me see the opportunity that I thought was outside my grasp. You'll always be my favorite, and not just because you wrote the Acknowledgements.

CHAPTER ONE

BASICALLY

I've always loved the word "basically". It's basically a word that I basically overuse and am often teased about—but basically, that doesn't affect my linguistic attraction to the word at all. But what does "basically" even mean? If I say I'm basically happy, does that imply actual happiness? Or am I perhaps saying that I'm mostly happy with a little bit of unhappiness? Am I stating that I'm happy for the most part? Then what about the least part? Basically, this word is a conundrum. A generalization, if you will. I might even go so far as to call it an enigma. Is "basically" even a basically honest word?

The other day, I basically heard someone say, "That was *basically* the funniest thing I had ever heard!" Basically, that's ironic. *Basically*, it was the funniest thing they had ever heard…but not really. Really?

"Basically" dumbs down the situation. It implies that what you're hearing is basically a summary. Basically, the essential parts are no longer essential. The word "basically" basically erases all of the details of a situation

3

and basically sugarcoats it.

Basically is basically dishonest. By saying that that thing was *basically* the funniest thing they had ever heard, they basically implied that there is someone or something funnier out there. How do I know? Look at the word *implied*. It says right there that you *lied*.

Some would basically consider it kind to imply, but do we really want to live in a society that basically *lies* and calls it sugar? Not me!

Some think that "basically" is an appropriate summary word. "Basically, my brother thinks I'm insane". But basically, by stating that, you ignore all the relevant details and force people to stereotype. You're basically on a one-person crusade to profile people. It's basically cruel. Basically, all I'm trying to say is that we should basically eradicate the term "basically" from our everyday language to avoid basically lying to each other in our attempts to basically make everyone feel funnier than they basically are. Except for me, because it's basically my favorite word.

BASICALLY

CHAPTER TWO

LIKE

If you've ever, like, been around teenagers, you like, know that they like totally overuse the term "like". It's basically, like, really distracting to like, listen to a teenager like talk to you because you like, find yourself like basically counting the "likes" and like lose track of what they're like trying to like, say. Like, really. It's obnoxious.

It's like almost awkward because it's like they keep trying to like make connections with things that are like totally unconnected. Like if someone were to say "a napkin is like a paper towel", then that's like totally and basically appropriate because, like, napkins and paper towels are like basically the same. But if they like say that "he like walked up to me and like started like talking about football," then that's like totally not like even okay. I basically don't like talking about football anyways. Like it's basically boring and I don't get it. Well, like I do get it, but that's like not the point. This guy like walking up to some girl is like so not like the same thing as him like talking about like football.

Make sense? Basically, it should.

Now there's like a whole other dimension to "like." I like hear people say stuff all the time, like, "I mean I like him, but not *like*-like him, 'cause it's like not like that." Like, what does that like even like mean? Is "like-like" like a double like, or is it like basically love? Do two likes make like more than just one like does? Or if I say "I *like* like him" does that like mean that I like like in a similar like, way as him? "Like" just like, causes so much like confusion in like relationships and all that. Basically, don't like overuse like. Even if you really like *like* like someone. Like seriously

There's even like a third dimension to "like". I like chocolate milk. It's like basically delicious. But if I like say "I like like chocolate milk" then it's like basically confusing because it like sounds like "I *like* like chocolate milk" which already has like so many different like meanings that it's like basically awkward. Like really.

BASICALLY

KATELYN DALTON

CHAPTER THREE

Y'KNOW

Y'know like when somebody is telling you something and they basically seem to like y'know, expect you to know something? Basically like even if you don't like actually know what they're talking about. Like y'know you basically have to say like you *do* know because they already basically, y'know, said that you know so like obviously you must know.

Y'know is almost...like...mean. Y'know what I mean? And not mean like y'know when I say like y'know what I mean mean, but mean like y'know not nice. When somebody, y'know, says, "y'know", then you know just to like nod because y'know you can't like question that they basically know that you know. You know like how it is.

And like even if you, y'know, don't, y'know, know, then you better like pretend you, y'know, know because...y'know. Like you just gotta, y'know, know.

"Y'know" is like a forceful word, because. Y'know, it

basically demands the other person to like agree to something even if, y'know, they don't, y'know, agree. Which, as I'm sure you know, can be incredibly, y'know, powerful, y'know, if you like are wanting to like basically mind control like everyone you, y'know, know.

BASICALLY

KATELYN DALTON

CHAPTER FOUR

LITERALLY

Ahh, literally. Literally is like y'know basically another lying word. I literally think that like everyone, y'know, who like basically uses like the word *literally* should literally be thrown in jail for like the rest of their lives, y'know? I like literally cannot stand it when the term "literally" is literally used basically, y'know, incorrectly.

Like for example, my friend was basically, y'know, like telling me about this boy. She like said, "Like I literally could not stop staring at him."

Literally? Like unless your eyes were literally surgically locked in a fixed point, y'know, and like basically directed at this boy, and like your head was basically like held in place with like, y'know, spikes or angry hornets, then like you are literally lying.

Liar. The overuse of the word "literally" like literally makes my head like basically feel like it is being crushed by like a million tiny hammers, y'know?

Now, y'know like on the other hand, if you were like basically describing an incident in which your heart literally stopped and you said like, "I literally died of, y'know, embarrassment," then like everyone would basically like literally breathe a sigh of relief at your refreshingly and, y'know, all too rare like correct use of "literally".

BASICALLY

KATELYN DALTON

CHAPTER FIVE

GOES

While "goes" may like seem like a word that would basically be difficult to misuse, y'know, today's society has like basically accepted that challenge. And they have like succeeded. Literally.

"Like she basically goes to the grocery store." This is like a correct, y'know, usage of the word. She traveled to a new location: the grocery store. (Why isn't like the past tense of *goes* something that is basically easier to remember, like *goed*? That would like literally save my life when I'm writing like, y'know, English papers.)

However, the modern teenager goes, "Like the weather is basically, y'know, gorgeous outside today." Hearing this is like literally worse to me than having my nose hairs plucked with like rusty tweezers. This like horrible misuse of the language basically makes me want to literally like pull my hair out. *She* does not go *anything* with the weather outside being like gorgeous. Like I've heard literally billions of conversations in which my friend goes "So Sarah, y'know, wanted like a smoothie, so she goes, 'Like I'll literally die if I don't like get a smoothie right now!' So she goes to that one place to get one and goes, 'There's like my major crush,' and he goes, 'Hey! Basically what are you doing here?' And she goes, 'Well I just like wanted a smoothie, and I'll like literally implode if I don't like get one basically in the next 30 seconds.' And he goes, 'Well you can go like anywhere you want now, 'cause like you got your license.' And y'know, she goes, 'Yeah, except basically only when my parents let me like borrow the car.' And then she has to go so he goes, 'I'm like going home,' and then like he goes home, and she like basically goes to the movies but then later he like texts her and goes, 'So we should literally hang out!' And like she calls me and goes, "He's so like awesome and literally the cutest boy on the planet,' and I go, 'Well y'know, you should basically text him back.' So she goes and texts him back, and goes, 'Yeah, totally.' Then they like go and basically make plans and then literally the next day they go out to lunch."

Did you get that?

BASICALLY

CHAPTER SIX

YOLO

Basically like literally the best thing about being a teenager in like the year 2013, which, y'know,' is the way we can basically make our parents and other like grown ups literally insane with acronyms that like they have never heard of.

YOLO is one of those. Basically the first time I like heard someone go "YOLO," I literally thought my friend was going, "Hello," but like she was trying to be basically funny. I literally died of embarrassment when my friend goes, "Like *everyone* knows what YOLO means. Y'know, you're literally living in a cave if you don't know YOLO.

Basically, YOLO means like "You Only Live Once," which is literally the most inspiring words on the planet. Y'know, *You Only Live Once* is like too long to say, so people will just go, "YOLO," instead of going, "You Only Live Once."

My favorite uncle like visited a couple months ago, and like he goes, basically, "I'm a hot shot, because like I wrote a book." and I go, "I want to, y'know, write a book too," and he goes, "basically I will help you," and I go, "YOLO!" He goes, "You can have a yellow book if you want," and I go, "No. Not like *yellow*, but YOLO."

He goes, "YOLO? I don't understand you silly teenagers these days," and I go like, "If you help me, I'll literally tell everyone you're my favorite uncle ever, and like you'll basically rock, and I'll even tell you what YOLO means." So he goes, "I'll basically help you," and I go, "YOLO means, 'You Only Live Once.'" Then he goes, "You rock, Katelyn, and now he's like literally my favorite uncle.

Ever.

ABOUT THE AUTHOR

Katelyn Dalton has loved looking at words, reading words, and writing words ever since she learned the alphabet. She like literally loves words to death. She's basically 16, though she literally refers to herself as 16 ½. Katelyn lives in Mechanicsville, Virginia, with her parents and three siblings. She overuses words all the time, and she's secretly entertained when she does. This is the first book. that she has written, and her favorite book that she has read.

Printed in Great Britain
by Amazon